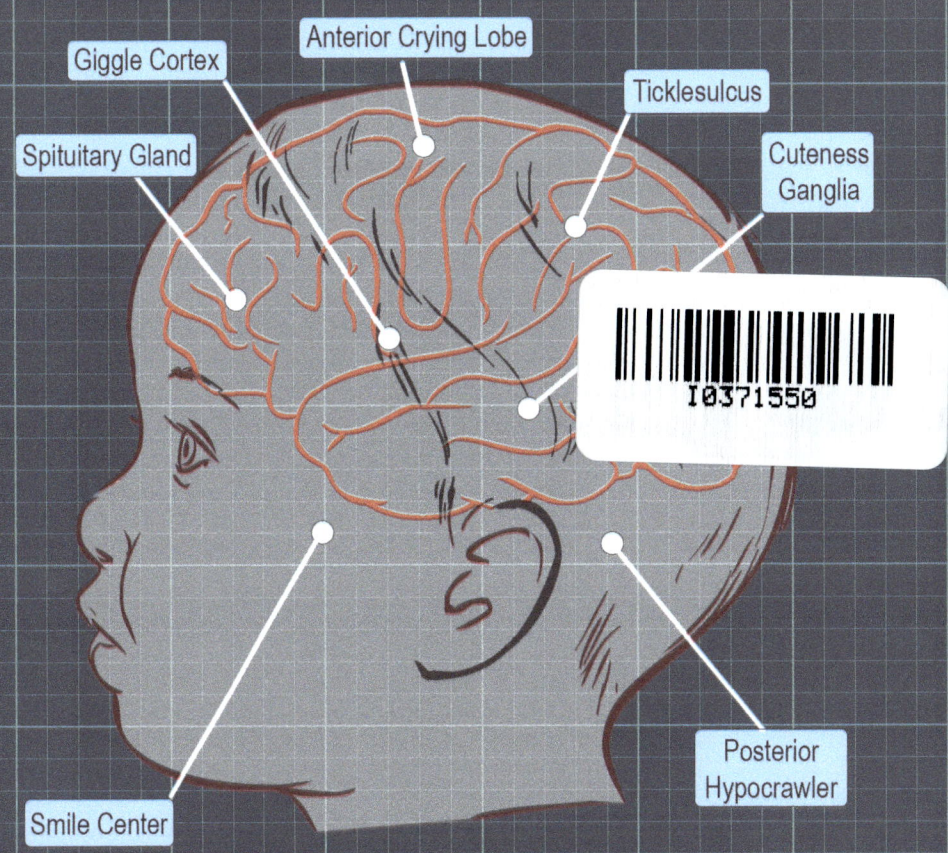

Baby's First Instruction Manual

How To Be the Center of the Universe

Jimmy Huston

Copyright © 2021 Jimmy Huston

ISBN: 978-1-970022-58-2

All rights reserved, including the right to use or reproduce this book or portions thereof in any form whatsoever without written permission from the publisher except in the case of brief quotations embodied in critical articles or reviews.

All images are used under license from Shutterstock.com

Cosworth Publishing
21545 Yucatan Avenue
Woodland Hills CA 91364
www.cosworthpublishing.com

For information regarding permission,
please send an email to office@cosworthpublishing.com.

For Casey

who is already the center of the universe.

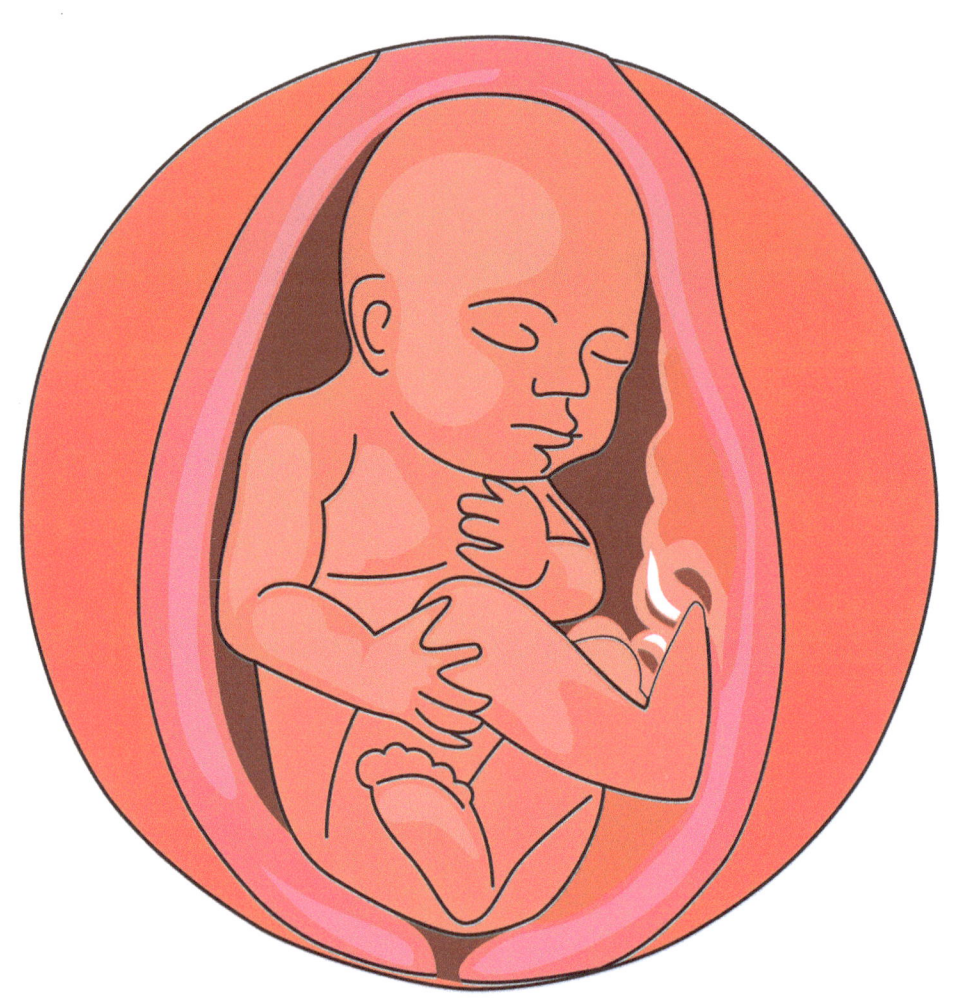

Welcome

You've been a fetus long enough.

After nine months in the dark, it all may seem too bright.

And, you're going to hear a lot more noise than you're used to *in utero.* That noise is coming mostly from your parents.

If you want the sound to stop, simply close your eyes. Then you'll hear a lot of *shhhhhhhhing* -- and people shout-whispering, 'Quiet! The baby's sleeping!'

If it's still too loud and you want *all* the noise stopped, close your mouth. That sound is *you* -- crying.

By the way, that warm, soft thing you've been lying on is your mom. Let her rest. She's had a stressful night.

You'll be learning about her later. She will explain a lot of things to you.

But for now, get someone to turn the page for you.

Chapter One

First Things First

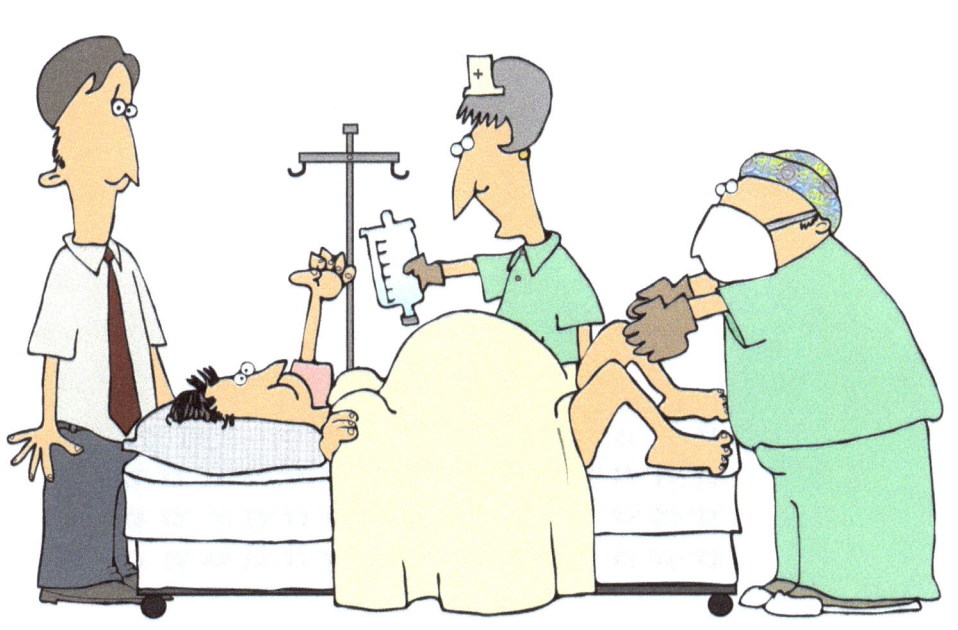

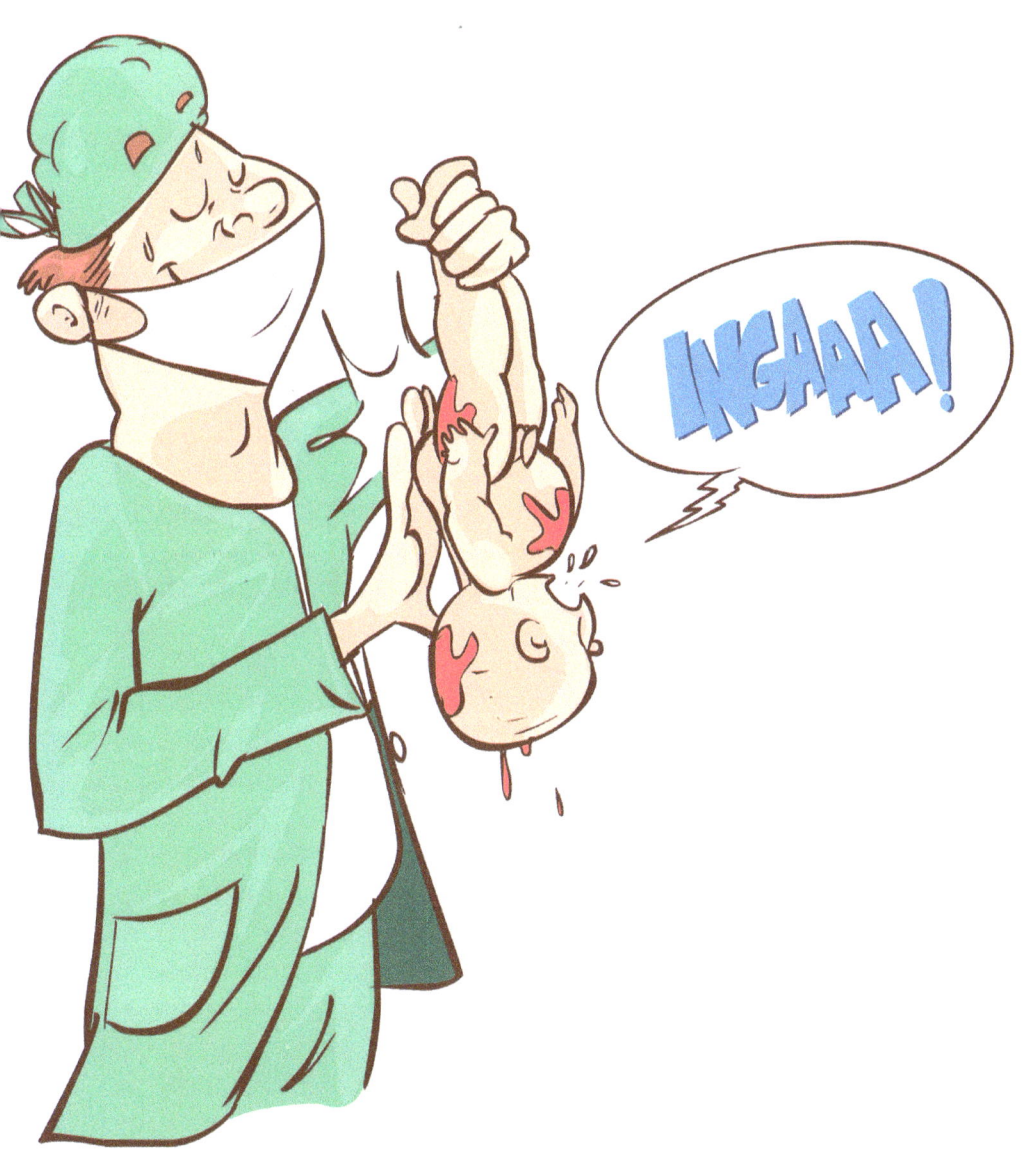

BREATHE

And breathe again. And again. And again. And again.

And again. And again. And again. And again. And again. And again. And again. And again. And again. And again. And again. And again. And again. And again. And again.You'll get used to it. And again. It gets easier. Really. And again. Whatever you do, don't dare stop! And again. And again. And again. And again. And again. And again. And again. And again. And again. You're finally getting it. And again. And

again. And again. Etc., etc., etc. etc. etc.

Suck

You may not have noticed, but there's no more umbilical cord. That means the free ride is over.

Luckily, there is an alternative. That 'mom' mentioned earlier was your feedbag -- a handy source of food, energy, protein, vitamins, etc. -- and, she still is, but now you're going to have to go after it.

She is a miraculous fountain of sustenance. What you need to look for is... well, she's probably going to help with this, and you'll probably find three meals a day right in your face. Just clamp down and enjoy.

Sucking is a lot like breathing -- which you mastered on the previous page -- except that instead of air, you've got a deliciously sweet liquid coming in.

And, instead of inhaling into your lungs and then blowing it out, you'll swallow it into your stomach.

(Don't ask where it goes after that or you might lose your appetite. You'll be learning that stuff soon enough.)

Cry

It's just another form of breathing -- only more urgent.

But, it's your most powerful tool. People will come running from all directions. 'Are you hungry?' 'Are you wet?' 'What do you want?'

Until, eventually, it doesn't seem to work any more. But don't give up. Keep crying!

In time, Mom and Dad will do *anything* to stop it.

They'll ply you with goodies to eat. They will take you for a ride. They'll rock you till they drop. It's great fun!

Pee

It's not hard. Just stop *not* peeing.

Just let go. Relax. Enjoy the comforting warmth.

You'll soon discover that peeing provides unlimited entertainment as you watch those around you react, scrambling to get out of the line of fire.

You'll learn about timing -- particularly comic timing. Obviously, the best time to pee is during a diaper change.

Boys will learn about target practice.

Girls will simply tinkle.

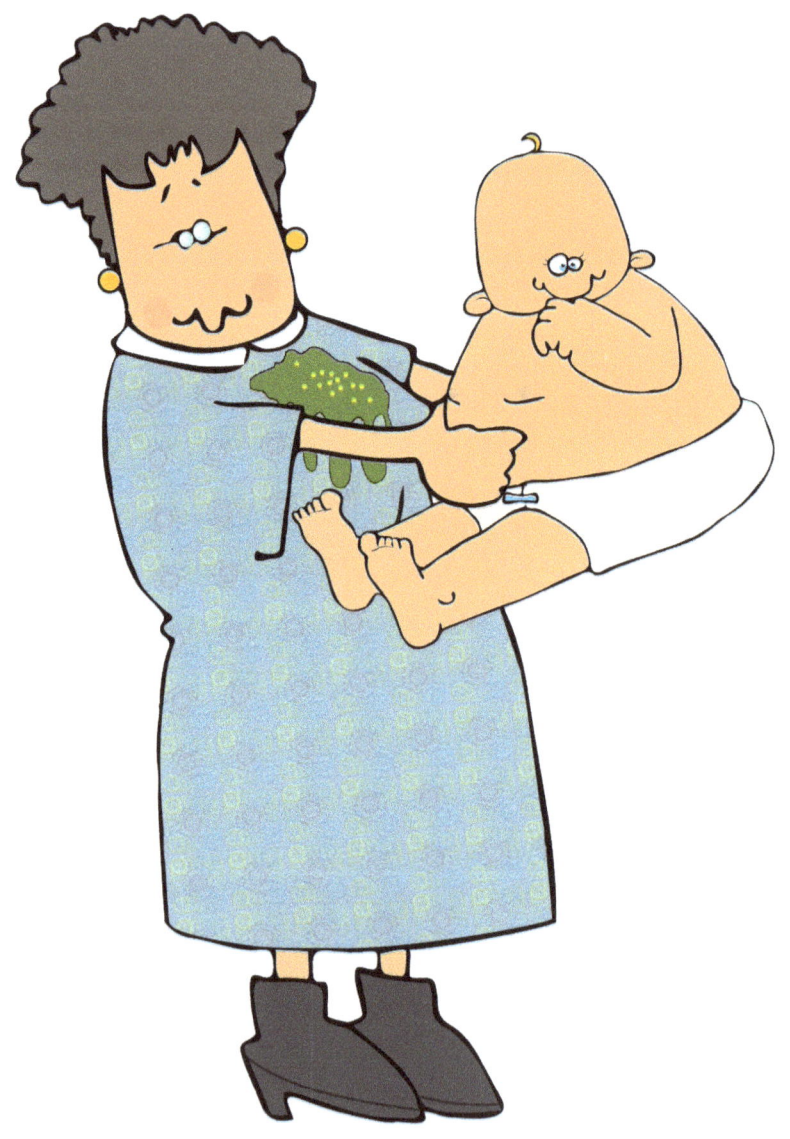

Spit Up

Eventually you're going to get tired of being passed around between grownups who all want to 'hold the baby.'

The quickest way to put a stop to that is to spit up -- preferably on someone's dressy outfit. Silk is good. Or cashmere.

Remember, it's about timing, not quantity or distance.

Reactions will range from 'ehhh' to 'horrific,' but oddly enough, no one will blame you. They all know they should have known better.

It's not hard to spit up. It's just one more version of breathing, but this time there's a little bit of whatever you're digesting. That adds color, texture, and aroma to things.

And stains. Enjoy.

Poop

Not your fault, right? It just shows up somehow -- never where you're looking. It's always a surprise.

And it's always changing. Not just in consistency, but in both velocity and bouquet.

Afterwards, you'll feel bouncy and energized. If you'd like to tell the world, but you can't talk, perhaps some special pooping noises will highlight the moment.

In general, an impressive poop will get you a lot of attention, especially from Mom.

Dad, however, will be handing you off to whoever's closest.

The best time to poop is right after you get a fresh diaper, which is pretty often, so if one try doesn't work, don't worry. You'll get another chance soon enough.

And, it doesn't matter where you are -- church, the grocery store, or in the car on a long trip. Just poop away and enjoy.

Luckily, poop is a renewable, never-ending resource. Miraculously, you'll never run out.

Chapter Two

FAMILY

Mom

The good one.

Not only is she delicious, but she's wonderfully helpful, too.

She'll be providing you all the necessities and teaching you things along the way. Mom will nurse you tirelessly when you're sick or hurt. She will play ball with you. Someday she will dance with you. Whatever you want to do, Mom will find a way.

She will teach you to sing. Or sew. Or garden. Or swim. Or dig a gold mine. Or build a spaceship. She will even take you fishing, if you insist. She is the perpetual playdate.

And she never leaves.

You will never understand the sacrifices your mom has made for you along the way.

You -- the child she adores -- have given her cramps, acne, migraines, diarrhea, abdominal pains, morning sickness, hemorrhoids, insomnia, contractions, and stretch marks.

None of it matters to her. Your mom just doesn't complain. (At least not yet. That day may come, but it's far away.)

Before you were born -- before even *she* was born -- they were already writing songs about her. And poems, too. Loving lyrics about the mother she is becoming.

When she was a little girl, her thoughts were already about you -- and here you are.

It's magic. It's fate. It's the most important relationship in your young life.

All you have to do in return is -- every now and then -- flash her your best grin. That's the smile she lives for.

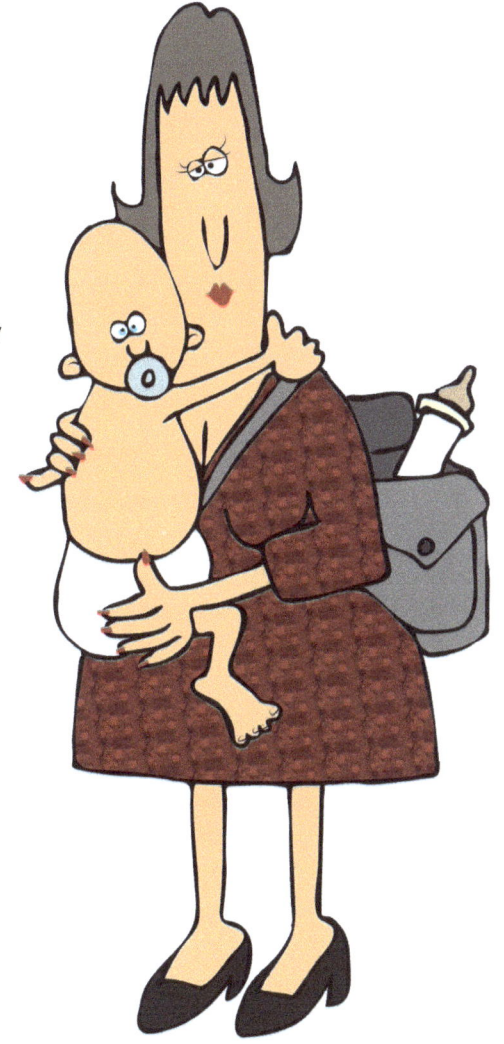

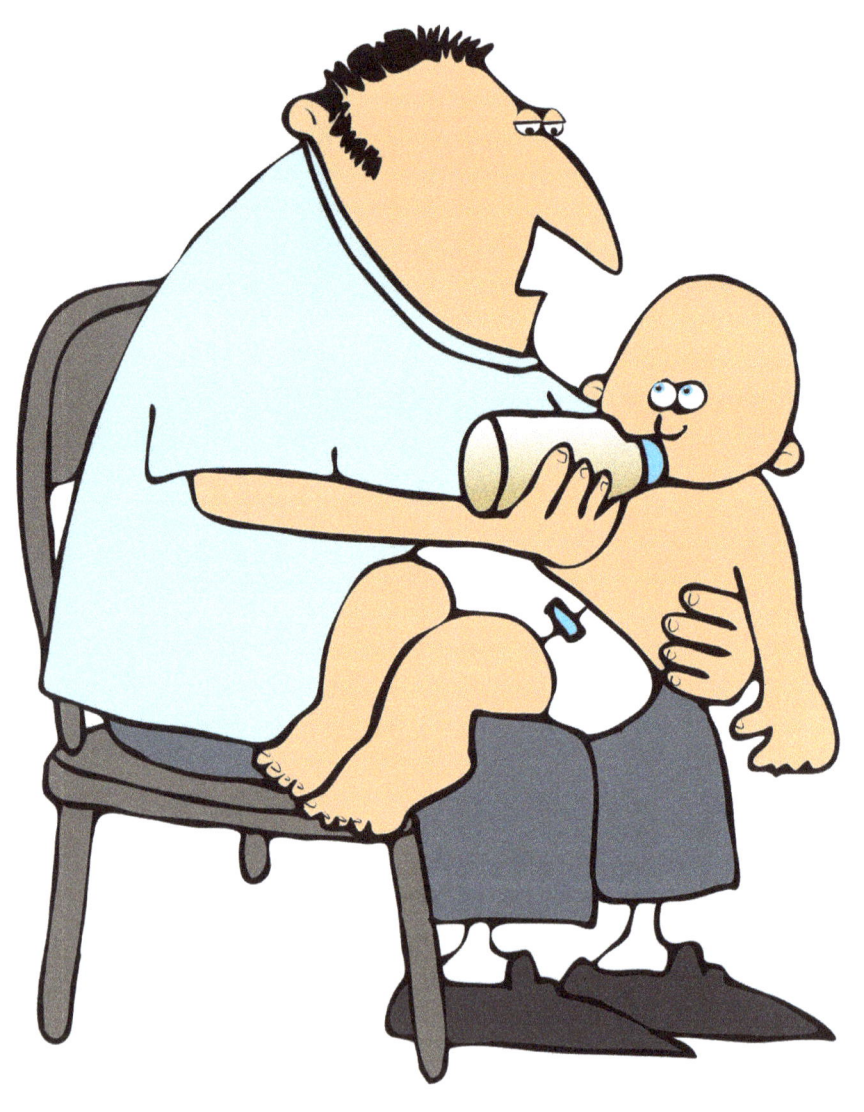

Dad

The other one -- the loud one -- is your dad.

Ehhhhhh... he cares, and he tries, but you're right -- it's not the same.

There aren't many songs about dads -- for good reason. Instead, moms get all the attention -- for good reason.

Dad is no good at all for nursing. He's almost useless for changing diapers. He's not always home when he should be. He thinks he's in charge of everything. And he snores!

An unlikely bundle of odd smells and sounds, he will teach you things, but much of it will be wrong. Some will just be inappropriate. Whenever you get in trouble, it will usually be his fault.

He will play the wrong music and buy you the wrong gifts. Don't let him teach you to parallel park.

He must be tolerated, but you'll find some consolation knowing that someday you'll be able to put him in a home.

Siblings

Oh, boy. Or girl.

Either one is a mixed blessing.

Sometimes they're older (ouch!).

Sometimes they're younger.

Neither is ideal.

Sometimes they're boys.

Sometimes they're girls.

Neither is ideal.

But you're stuck. And for a long, long, long time.

You will learn from each other, and *despite* each other.

Together, you will learn about competition. Grudgingly, you will even learn about cooperation.

You will become reluctant lifetime allies in the ongoing war with Mom and Dad.

There will be good times and hard times, but your siblings will always be there -- trying to get an edge.

Perhaps the worst thing you will learn together is 'sharing.' There will be stories, examples, parables, and such, but all will be in vain. Sharing is a crock.

You're not allowed to kill each other, but everything else is fair game.

Grandparents

Don't worry. They're harmless, despite the endless squeezing.

They come from the past. And, they may smell a little different, but they can be quite useful. Whenever Mom or Dad say 'no,' go crying to Grandma. You'll get your way.

There are lots of traditional names for grandparents: gramps, bubbie, grandpaw, granny, papa, nana, gramma, meemaw, gammy, grimps, etc.

But you -- who can't even talk -- get to make up your own names for them. Whenever you see either grandparent, simply shout a weird noise. Do it enough times and that weird sound will become the official name of that grandparent. Try it!

They have endless stories. Unfortunately it's not an endless variety. It's the same stories over and over again.

Your parents have known them for a long, long time, and they are afraid that your grandparents will try to buy your affection with candy, treats, and toys. You should let them.

It's for their own good.

Babysitters

These temporary parental substitutes may entertain you, or ignore you, or teach you things your parents don't want you to know. They will certainly have better music than you usually hear.

They may ask you what you want to play, but they don't mean it. They're going to do what they want to do.

Good, bad, or indifferent, they all have one thing in common. At the end of the day, or evening, they are going home.

What a relief...

Pets

They're like family, almost family, but not *quite* family.

They're animals. Cute, furry, and unpredictable. They may lick you. Or bite you. Or scratch you.

Pets come in all sizes, shapes, and colors. They sometimes make strange noises. Some of them can even fly. Others live underwater. They all smell, so you'll have something in common.

In fact, they will be fascinated by your odor, so love them, but be careful. Before you came along, they were higher in the family pecking order. Now they're not.

Also, pets are unusually attracted to all of the various things that come out of you, so don't lick or put in your mouth anything that comes out of them.

Chapter Three

Necessaries

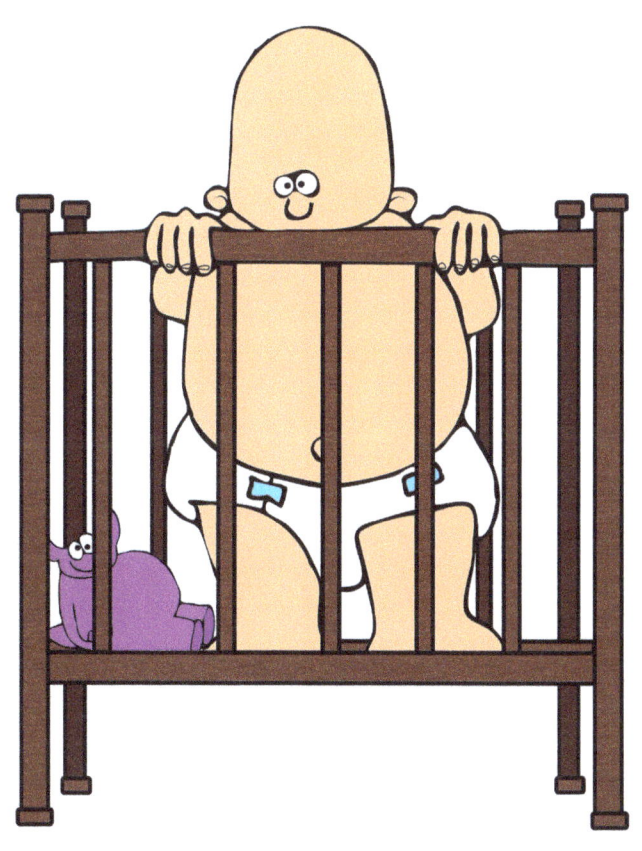

Diapers

They keep the floor clean. That's good.

But not you.

With diapers, wherever you go, you'll be dragging around all your pee and poop, often leaving a trail like a slug.

As hard as you work to fill the diapers, your mom and dad will be dumping them behind your back.

And, for some reason, when you're wearing diapers your parents will be constantly sniffing around you like they're digging for truffles. They wish.

You should know that after a couple of free-wheeling diaper years where anything goes, *anywhere,* the diapers go away.

You'll be expected to stop pooping and peeing -- except in certain special rooms, usually at inconvenient times of someone else's choosing.

It will not go well.

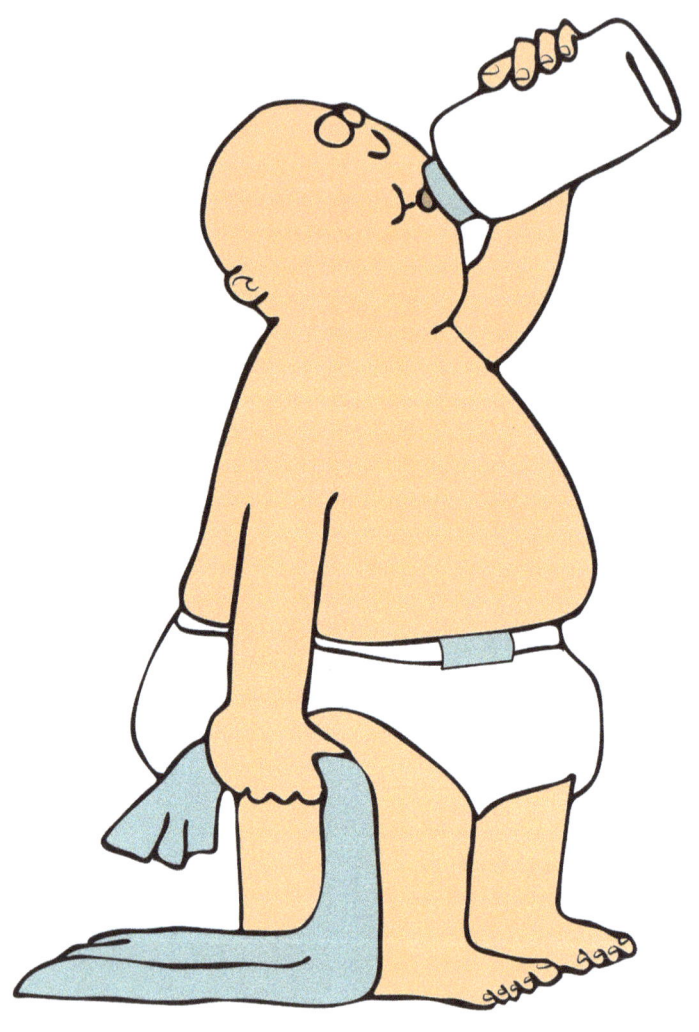

BOTTLES

Do not trust them. They are trying to replace your mom.

Anyone, even your dad, can hand you a bottle.

It's critical that you don't allow it. Do not take a bottle from anyone, anywhere, under any circumstances.

Unless you're hungry.

They're hard, usually plastic, and they don't rock you or sing to you like Mom.

They do come in more flavors and a variety of temperatures, so that's good. (Mom can't produce fruit juice.)

Boycott the bottles. Hang onto Mom while you can.

Pacifiers

Pacifiers are a lie.

They are not what they pretend to be. And they're empty. Suck all you like, but nothing will come out. All you can really do is throw them as far as you can. Try it!

Like most imitation products, these 'plugs' are nothing like the real thing. They are a preliminary form of addiction, allowing parents to withhold or allow -- depending on your behavior.

Remember, the worse you behave, the more likely you'll be bribed with a binky.

Baths

Totally useless.

Why get clean? It's not like you're going to *stay* clean.

But, baths are obligatory, so make the best of it. Baths can be fun. See how far you can splash the water. If *you* have to be wet, *everybody* gets wet.

Also, with the diaper out of the way, it's a great time to pee or poop!

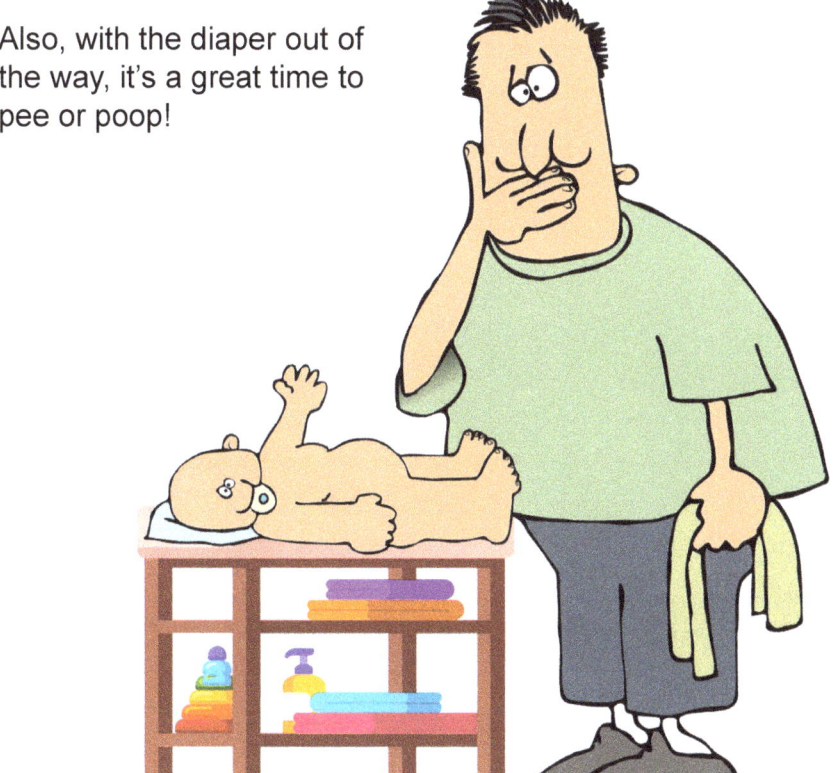

Food

You're probably wondering, 'What's wrong with breastfeeding? Was I complaining?'

One thing has changed. Teeth. If you're going to chew, you're going to need real food -- not Mom!

Real food can be fun. You can drool it all over yourself and anyone close. Spit it as far as you can. Smear it everywhere. Paint the walls with it. Drop it on the floor. Throw it at visitors. Be creative. Go wild!

Or, you can swallow it.

The food they will offer you is generally tasteless. It certainly needs salt. It also changes your poop, and not for the better.

But, get used to it. You really can't go back to Mom.

That's why she's trying sooooo hard to get you to eat it, making all those silly faces and sounds. Make her happy.

Gum it and swallow. It'll be coming back around one way or another. Both of you can enjoy it again and again.

Someday there will be pizza, but until then -- mush.

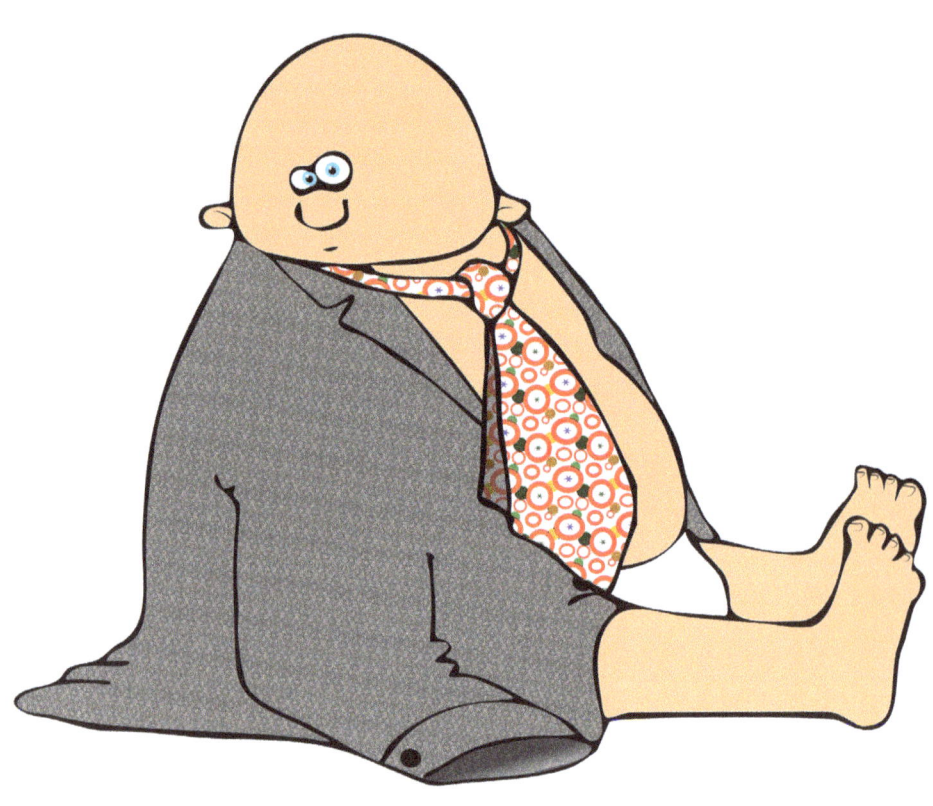

CLOTHING

Ridiculous.

Yes, indeed, but clothes are definitely coming your way. Whether the weather is cold or hot, you'll be getting all dressed up, kiddo.

It's your mom's way of playing with dolls. She will dress you up with all the exquisite and ridiculously impractical baby clothes people have been giving you.

Even if they fit (which they won't), they won't fit for long.

Feel free to excrete all over them in whatever manner seems the easiest.

CARSEATS

Maybe you're under arrest. That's the only thing that makes any sense.

You're immobilized, strapped into the back seat and facing backwards. You're a prisoner, being transported to who knows where, without your consent, and unable to communicate.

In the carseat you're subjected to a puzzling variety of motion sensations -- forward, backward, accelerating, leaning, and braking. No wonder it makes you carsick.

You need a lawyer.

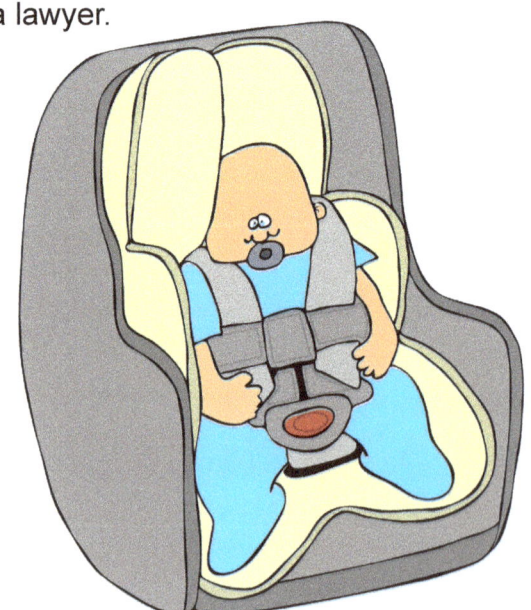

Strollers

It's your very first vehicle. You'll probably notice that it doesn't have brakes. Or steering. And there's no accelerator.

Magically you just lurch forward, wheeling around maniacally as you careen toward looming obstacles, dreading the crash.

There's always someone following right behind you. Why don't they do anything?

It's frightening to constantly veer around things at the last second with no control whatsoever and no assurance that the next time won't be a horrific collision.

You need a lawyer.

Chapter Four

Health

Doctors

They call themselves pediatricians, which is a big word for something or other. Who cares?

They are there to take care of you, to keep you healthy, and to help you grow.

You can't trust them.

They are going to poke you and prod you and stick you. They will prescribe things that taste horrible. And, they will peer into places they have no business looking. No orifice is safe from doctors.

They'll weigh you, measure you, listen to your heart, check your blood pressure, look in your ears -- then ask your mom how you feel.

They're way too interested in pee, poop, puke, snot, boogers and your *blood!* **Your blood!**

That's it! Pediatrician means vampire!

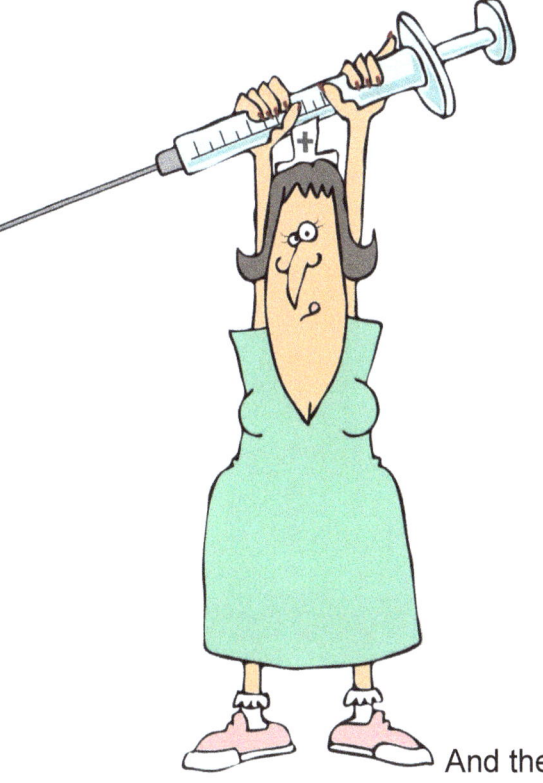

And the nurses aren't much better.

Circumcision

Girls:

You can skip this page.

But you won't.

Boys:

Ask away. You'll never get a straight answer about this.

And, you'll never get to vote on it. No one cares what you think.

Just accept it and move on.

They'll say it's for your own good. For your health. And then, somewhere out of your view, there will be snickering.

Depending on your religion, you might get a sip of wine out of this, but a sip is not going to be enough.

Another thing they won't tell you -- it's for the girls.

Huh?

Chapter Five

Growing Up

Teething

You were born with all your teeth already in your head.

Not in your mouth. In your head.

In time they will 'erupt' through your gums. That's right. They will essentially chew their way through your young, strong, ultra-sensitive gums. It's going to hurt.

All you can do is make everyone around you just as miserable as you are. Make them pay.

Cry, cry, cry, cry, cry, cry, cry. And then cry some more.

CRAWLING

Sitting is boring. Lying down is even worse. Wouldn't it be fun to go over there...?

Hmmmm....

This is how all the trouble starts -- with locomotion.

So push. Kick. Even roll. Somehow you'll start to move. Push with your legs. Grab with your hands. Scoot, scoot, scoot.

It's not elegant, but suddenly the whole house is within reach.

There are dog toys, trash cans, bookshelves, coffee tables, kitchen cabinets, and electrical outlets -- an endless array of trouble to get into.

All are better than the dumb plastic toys in your crib. Go for it!

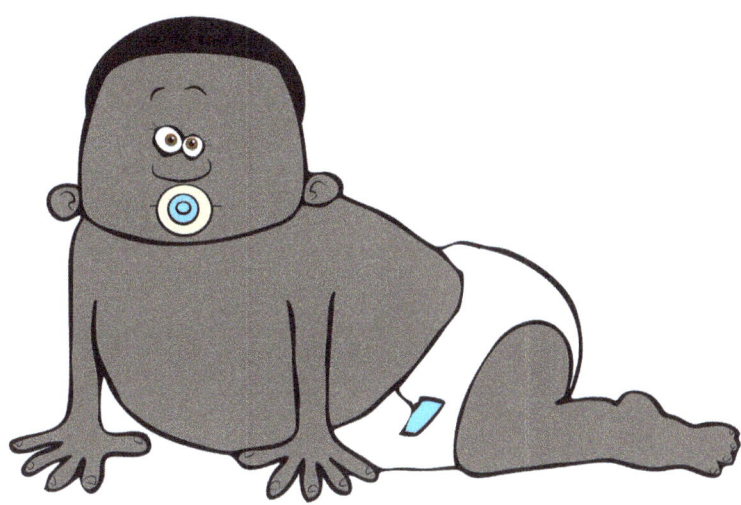

Toilet Training

It turns out that diapers aren't the answer after all.

Instead of being limited to soiling a small square of paper or cloth, now you get an entire room to mess up.

1. Boys: you get to stand while peeing. Eventually, you'll learn to pee in the toilet. Until then just spray the room, marking your territory for the world to see.

    Oh, and if anyone is watching, lift the seat before you pee. Otherwise...

    Girls: see number 2.

2. Have a seat. Don't fall in. You may have to sit there for a while.

    Go.

    Wipe.

When you're finished, take one last look at what you've been creating.

Say goodbye.

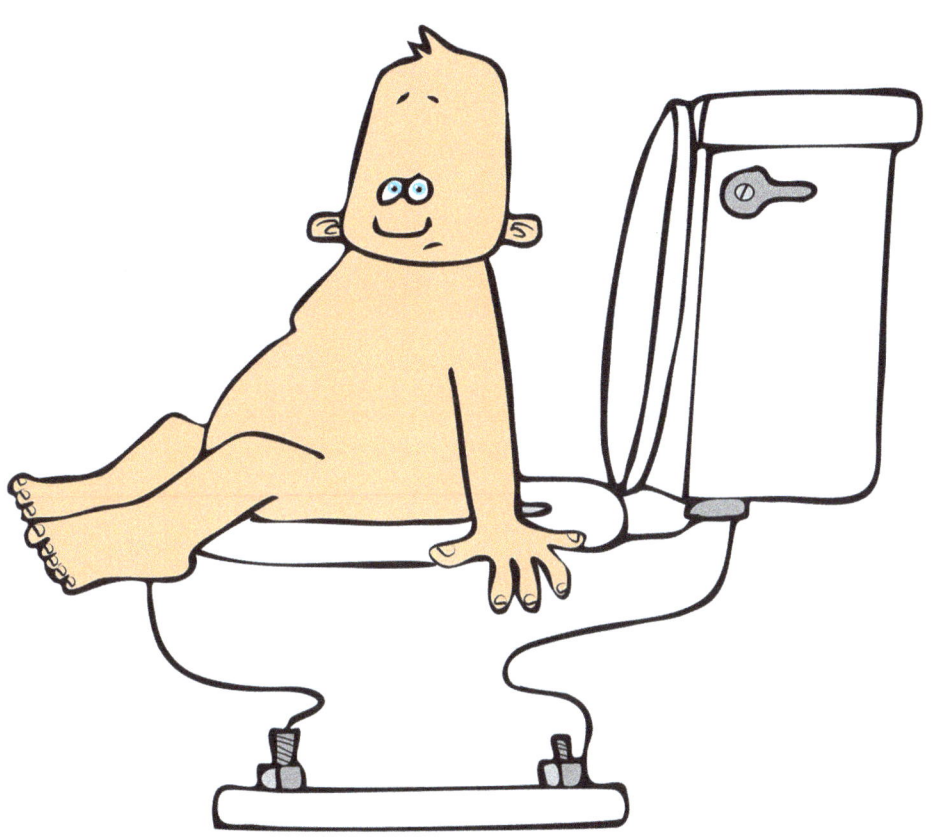

Flushing is a great fun activity. It's a loud form of magic where you can make things disappear forever -- or at least until the plumber comes to retrieve them.

Boys get to brag about what they've done.

Girls quietly deny it all.

Talking

If you breathe a certain way, noises come out of your mouth. Your mom and dad do it all the time, right in your face.

Some of these noises refer to certain people or things. Others mean actions or activities.

If you can match the sounds your mom and dad make, everyone will get really excited and say that you're smart.

Talking is more specific than just crying, so it's a better way to get your mom and dad to meet your demands.

WALKING

This is going to hurt, but it's worth it.

Get used to falling -- a lot.

First, pull yourself up on something. Once you're up, lean until you start to fall forward. Then swing a leg out in front to catch yourself. Push against it and get your balance.

If you're still standing, try it again with the other leg. Lean, swing, catch yourself. Over and over.

Everyone is going to cheer you on. Then they'll prevent you from going where you want to go, guiding you to the most boring spots in the room.

Just wait. Your time will come.

Once you can walk,
the world is yours.

Chapter Six

In Conclusion

LAUGH

Another breathing thing. Another weird noise.

But this one means you're happy. It will even make you feel happy. It will make everyone around you happy, too.

You will quickly learn to giggle, chortle, snicker, and guffaw.

And that will help you get whatever you want.

In addition, if you're tired of all the constant peeing and pooping and spitting up, over and over again, there's good news.

You haven't really noticed, but you've slowly been growing -- ever-so-slightly. You're bigger now, and smarter. That's going to continue, and with it comes the ability to do and understand more things.

There will still be lots of peeing and pooping, of course, but there will be better things to do between the poops and pees. You'll be playing better games, meeting non-siblings, eating new foods, and someday experimenting with new drinks.

But, no matter how big you grow or how much you learn, you are still going to be spending much of your day peeing and pooping.

So laugh it up.

And remember all of this. Someday, you may have a baby of your own!

About the Author

Jimmy Huston is a native of Athens, Georgia, who lives in Woodland Hills, California with his wife and dog. A sometime screenwriter and filmmaker, he claims that he once was a baby, too. His daughters aren't so sure.

Other odd children's books from Jimmy Huston
www.byjimmyhuston.com

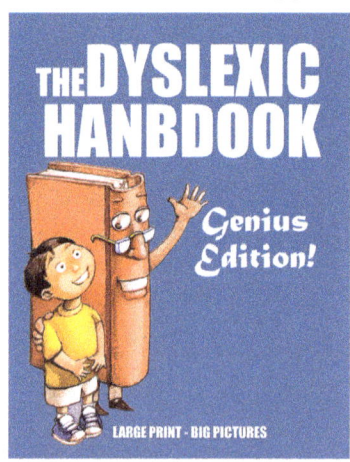

More books from Jimmy Huston
www.cosworthpublishing.com

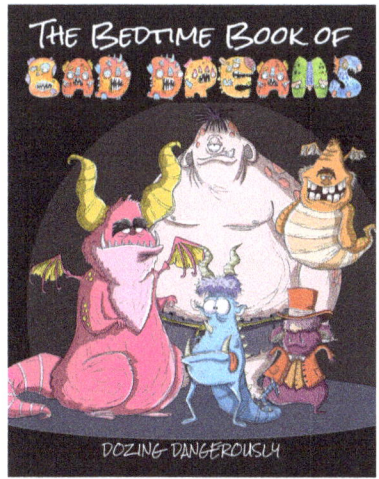

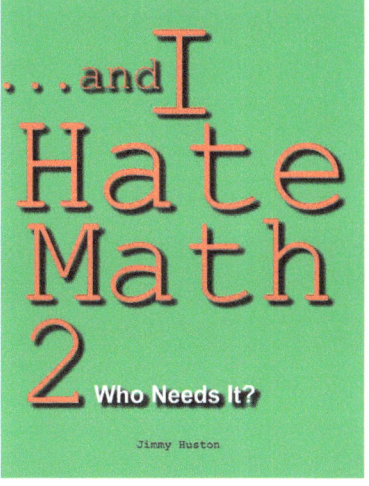

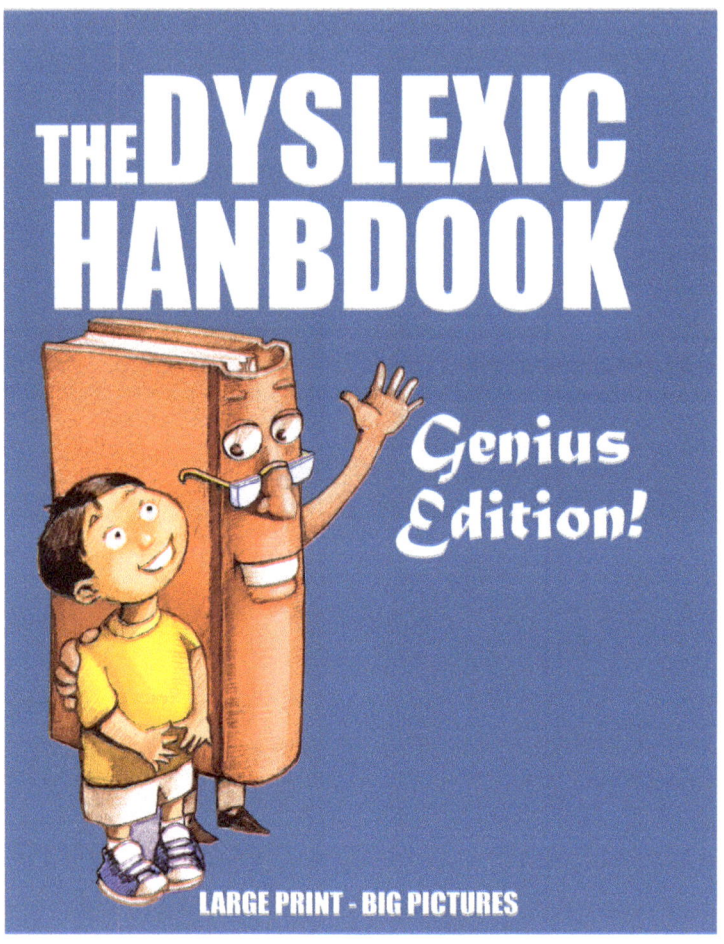

Who* buys a book for a kid with dyslexia?

Giving a self-help book to a dyslexic kid is like offering a drink of water to someone who is drowning.

So, have someone read it to you, so you can listen and think about it — and look at the pictures.

This book is also available as an audiobook.
(You'll have to imagine the pictures.)

* Someone who cares.

Other books from Cosworth Publishing
www.cosworthpublishing.com

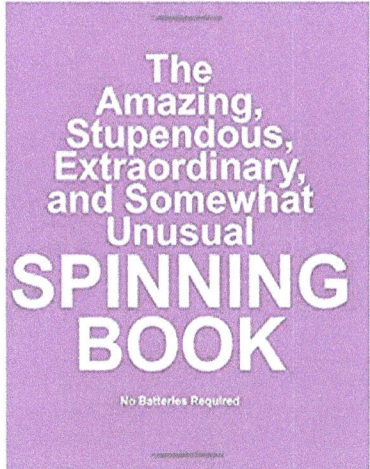
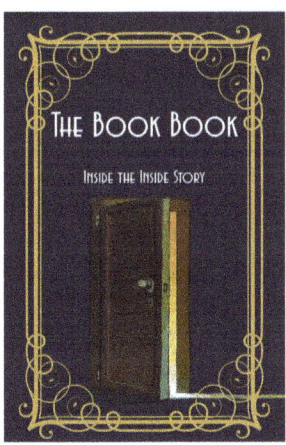

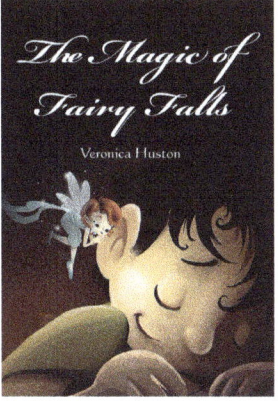
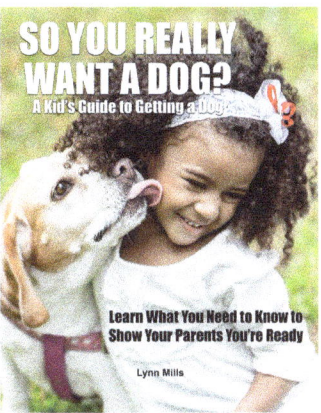

Find it wherever good books are dreaded.

If you're reading this, you will not like this book. It's not for you.

This book is for all the people who are *not* reading this.

They won't like it either, but it's short.

They'll like that.

"I didn't actually read this book. If I had, I would have loved it — but I never will."   Billy

"Hate isn't a strong enough word for me. I loathe reading. I don't even like looking at pictures - which there are none of."   Wally

"This isn't what I wrote about this stupid book."   Zane

"This is an excellent coffee table book, if your coffee table hates to read."   Solomon

"This book made my teacher cry."   David

"My son loved this book. He said it was delicious."   Mr. Jones

"THIS BOOK IS SO DUMB THAT I COULD'VE WRITTEN IT."   Jimmy

www.cosworthpublishing.com

Other books from Cosworth Publishing
www.cosworthpublishing.com

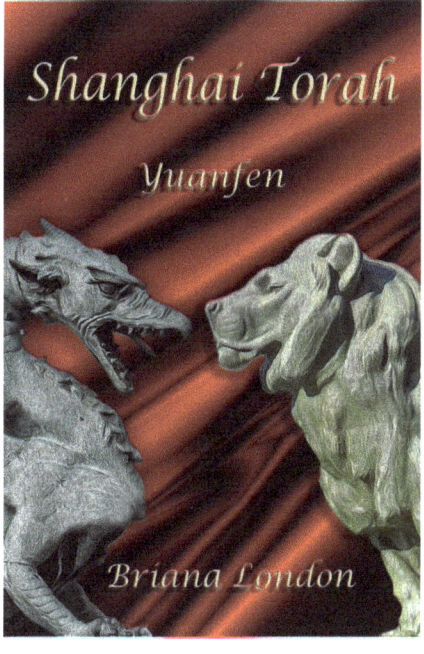

Also Available from Cosworth Publishing
www.cosworthpublishing.com

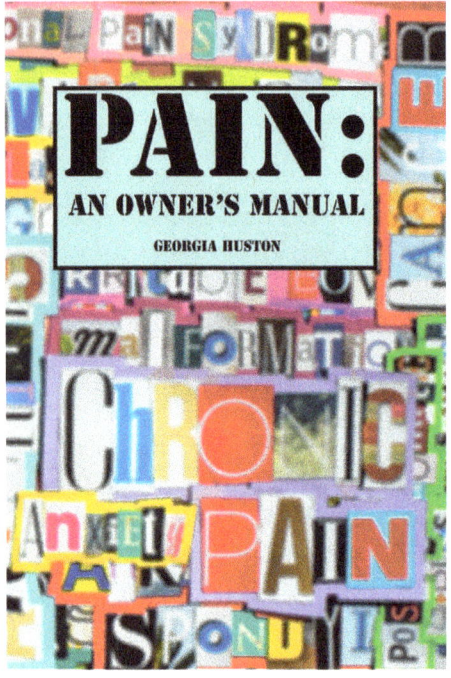

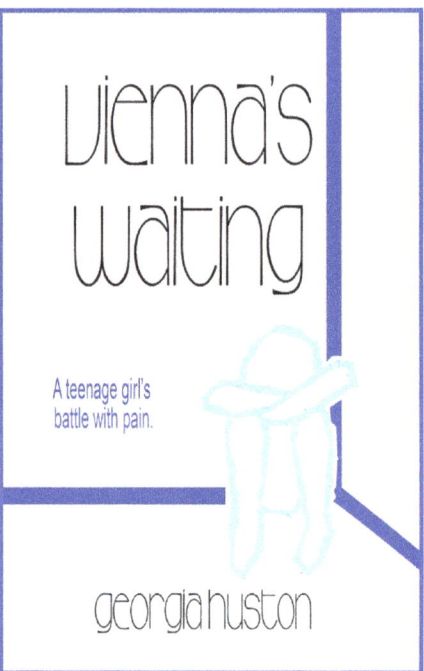

**Thanks for buying, borrowing,
or swiping this book.**

At Cosworth Publishing we truly appreciate that, and in return, we'd like to offer you one of our E-books absolutely free—and worth every penny.

Just let us know that you want it, and we'll make sure that you get it. Send an email to
office@cosworthpublishing.com.

Then, from time to time, we will let you know via email when we have a new book that you might be interested in.

We won't do that very often because we're basically pretty lazy, and we don't produce very many new books.

Reviews are greatly appreciated.